DATE DUE

Action Sports

Sumo Wrestling

Bill Gutman

Capstone Press

MINNEAPOLIS

Printed in the United States of America.

Capstone Press • 2440 Fernbrook Lane • Minneapolis, MN 55447

Editorial Director   John Coughlan
Managing Editor   John Martin
Production Editor   James Stapleton
Copy Editor   Thomas Streissguth

Library of Congress Cataloging-in-Publication Data

Gutman, Bill.
   Sumo wrestling / Bill Gutman.
      p.   cm.
   Includes bibliographical references and index.
   Summary: Describes the ancient Japanese art and sport of
sumo including the rules, preparation, techniques, and
importance to the wrestler. Includes a glossary of terms.
   ISBN 1-56065-273-X
   1. Sumo--Juvenile literature.   [1. Sumo. 2. Wrestling.]
I. Title
GV1197.G88 1996
796.8'125--dc20   95-7105
                                                         CIP
                                                         AC

99 98 97 96 95   6 5 4 3 2 1

Table of Contents

Chapter 1

What is Sumo Wrestling?

Japanese sumo wrestling goes back thousands of years. There are records of sumo fighting in the year 23 B.C. Several hundred years ago, sumo was still a form of deadly combat.

Over the years, sumo became an art and a sport. It still had some military and religious importance. But it also became a popular athletic contest. Sumo champions were admired for their strength and skill all over Japan. Sumo is still a very popular sport in Hawaii as well as in Japan.

Today, Japanese sumo is both a professional and amateur sport. There are major tournaments held each year. The winners are national heroes, like football, baseball, and basketball stars in North America.

In the early 1980s, Hawaiian-born Jesse Kahualua became the first non-Asian to become a sumo champion. Kahualua is famous in Japan, but still hardly known in the United States or Canada. While sumo has never really been popular in western countries, it can be a fun way to get in shape and improve your skills for other sports.

Yokozuna Akebono, a Hawaiian sumo wrestler, signs pogs for his young fans.

Chapter 2

The Rules of Sumo

Sumo contestants wrestle in a round **ring** that is 15 feet (4.5 meters) in diameter. That means 15 feet across at any point. Unlike a boxing ring, there are no ropes. A circle painted directly on the mat marks out the space where the sumo match will take place.

In Japan, the traditional sumo platform is raised two feet (60 centimeters) off the ground. It is built of a special clay and covered with a thin layer of sand. The platform is square, with the ring in the middle. The ring is marked by a curved, basket-like material several inches high in the middle and about four inches (10 centimeters) wide.

It's tough to move a sumo wrestler, no matter how hard you try.

The object of a sumo match is simple. The winner is the wrestler who forces his opponent out of the ring, or forces him to touch the floor inside the ring with any part of his body above the feet.

Contestants push, pull, slap, **throw, trip,** or grapple. They may also grab the loincloth, or belt, that is wrapped around their waists four to seven times. This loincloth, called a **mawashi** in Japan, is about two feet wide and made of heavy silk.

Very Big Men

Most professional sumo wrestlers are huge men. There are no weight divisions. If a man weighing 150 pounds wants to be a professional sumo wrestler, he may have to

Each group of sumo wrestlers gives small chocolate figures to their supporters.

wrestle a man twice his weight. It's not easy for a 150-pound man to push a 300-pounder around.

Champion sumo wrestlers need a lot of weight to compete, and many of them look fat. They aren't. They are very bulky and very strong. They must have powerful legs and a low center of gravity. That's because balance is important. Even sumo wrestlers who appear to have a large stomach are all muscle.

Sumo wrestlers look fat, but they're all muscle.

Wrestlers wear colorful outfits during the ceremony that takes place before the day's matches.

The hips are the center of balance and leverage for the sumo wrestler, who must also use his weight, strength, flexibility, and speed to win. His strength and size make the professional sumo wrestler almost impossible to move–except by another sumo wrestler.

Amazing Strength

Sumo wrestlers often invite five or six men from the audience to come into the ring and try to push them over. Even when they work together, groups of average men find it very difficult to make a top sumo wrestler move even one inch.

There is one story about a sumo wrestler who stood in front of an army jeep. He braced himself and told the driver to step on the gas. The tires spun furiously, but the huge wrestler just stood his ground. The jeep could not move. (Don't try this at home.)

Some of the stories about sumo wrestlers may just be legend. But there is little doubt that sumo wrestlers are very big, strong men.

Becoming a Sumo Champion

In Japan, young men who want to become champion sumo wrestlers begin training while they are still teenagers. Many of them are from working families and are used to difficult physical work. They are already strong, especially in the legs.

At a shrine in Japan, the followers of a champion sumo wrestler (yokozona) take part in a New Year's ceremony.

Beginners will spend up to six months training in sumo. They learn all the basic techniques as well as some of the traditional rituals of the art. From there, they join a group of sumo wrestlers of different skill levels.

The younger wrestlers must start at the bottom. At first, they do many of the chores, including cleaning and cooking. They serve the huge meals that the veteran sumo wrestlers eat. As their wrestling skills improve, they begin working their way through the ranks.

Getting Better

There are four levels that a young sumo wrestler must work his way through. He enters various matches and tournaments. At the end of these tournaments, there are awards for

Champion wrestlers form a circle at the opening of a grand sumo tournament.

winning. There are also awards for showing the most skill and the most fighting spirit.

As young sumo wrestlers become better, fan clubs and wealthy patrons begin supporting them with gifts of money. Like athletes in the United States and Canada, wrestlers can also make commercials. And, of course, they receive money for winning matches.

All professional sumo wrestlers want to become **grand champions**. The few who succeed are heroes in Japan.

Major Tournaments

There are six grand sumo tournaments each year in Japan. Each tournament lasts 15 days, and every wrestler fights once a day with a different opponent. All matches begin in the morning, with the lowest ranked wrestlers going first. At the end of the day, the matches featuring the grand champions take place.

Wrestlers in the lower four ranks fight just seven matches during a tournament. Their goal is to work into the upper ranks so they can fight the full 15 matches. After each

**According to sumo tradition, wrestlers stomp their feet
to drive evil spirits from the ring before the match.**

tournament, the rankings of the wrestlers
change, depending on how well they have
done.

Chapter 3

What Sumo Can Mean To You

Sumo wrestling is not a big sport in North America. It is not studied as much as some other martial arts, such as karate and tae kwon do. But it can be a fun sport to try with your friends. It can also help improve your balance and strength.

For example, two sumo wrestlers pushing and driving and trying to force each other out of the ring are like two lineman charging off the line of scrimmage in a football match. Strength, balance, and footwork are the keys in both sports.

Sumo is also a sport with very few injuries. It is a good way to test your strength, power, and quickness against someone else. You can also learn the many different throws, trips, and twists used by sumo wrestlers.

Sumo matches are usually over very quickly, so you can take part in a large number of matches. You can match your skill against the same opponent or against different opponents.

The wrestlers need quick moves and fast reflexes to get an advantage and defeat their opponents.

Wrestlers try to get a low and balanced position when they face off in the ring.

By the time you finish, you will get a good workout while improving your balance, quickness, and coordination.

Getting Ready to Wrestle

If you want to try sumo wrestling, you must get into good physical condition. You certainly don't have to weigh 300 pounds like professional sumo wrestlers. You can try the

sport at whatever weight you happen to be. But, as with any sport, there is no substitute for being in shape.

Aerobic exercises give you stamina and allow you to work out for a longer time without getting tired. Running, bike riding, jumping rope, and swimming are aerobic exercises that will help get you ready for sumo wrestling and for most other sports.

Other exercises such as pullups, situps, and pushups will help. So will a program of weight training. Always begin weight training with advice from a coach or instructor.

Stretching

Much of a sumo wrestler's power and balance comes from the hips down. That means his legs must be very strong. They must keep the wrestler on his feet as a strong opponent tries to throw him down.

The legs must be flexible as well. How flexible? Professional sumo wrestlers can do a

Some sumo opponents are easier to handle than others.

split with their legs out to the sides, while laying on their stomachs and keeping their chins on the ground. They can then reach back and grab their ankles with their hands.

Not even many experienced dancers can do this kind of split. Although doing splits isn't necessary in sumo, anyone practicing sumo should do a good set of stretching exercises for the legs.

Wrestlers warm up before a bout.

The referee watches closely as two wrestlers try to force each other out of the ring.

A Sumo Match

Some professional sumo matches are over in just seconds. Very few last longer than a minute. The wrestlers make their first moves with explosiveness. That's why the matches usually end quickly.

Each match, or **basho**, has one referee, who stays in the ring. There are also five judges who watch from the side. Sometimes the judges have to decide whether a wrestler touched the mat or not, or if a rule has been broken. But most matches are decided by the wrestlers.

In Japan, there are certain sumo traditions. For instance, a wrestler will throw a handful of salt into the ring before he enters. This is meant to cleanse or purify the ring. When he enters the ring, a wrestler will hold his hands high, showing his palms. This shows everyone that he has no weapons and that the basho will be a fair fight.

He then lifts one leg high in the air and brings it down with a loud stomp. He repeats this with the other leg. This tradition started as a way to drive evil spirits from the ring.

Both wrestlers start from a crouching position. They bow to each other. The referee waits until both are breathing regularly. He then signals the start of the match.

During a tournament, the bow ceremony takes place at the end of each day.

Before a match, wrestlers throw handfuls of salt to purify the ring.

The First Charge

Opponents usually test each other immediately. They **charge** with all the energy they can muster. The first collision can be shattering. If one man gets the advantage from the first charge, he can drive his opponent right out of the ring.

The sumo must keep his balance during the charge. At the same time, he must also set himself so that he cannot be moved by his opponent's charge. Strength, balance, and positioning are all working at once.

If neither man wins the match in the first charge, both must move quickly. They can back off and charge again. Or they may just continue to push and drive. Sometimes they will try other moves, such as a slap or a throw, to win the match. The top wrestlers are so strong and so good that the slightest advantage will bring them a victory.

Chapter 4

Some Sumo Techniques

There are said to be 48 different maneuvers that a sumo wrestler can use to win a match. Each, of course, has some variations. Some of them are easier to do than others. We cannot describe all of them here. But there are some basic moves, besides power pushing, that you can try.

As a wrestler pushes against his opponent, he can suddenly wrap his arms around the other man. Then he can try to throw him down with a powerful thrust to the left or right. He can also take a quick step to the right or left

According to the rules, a sumo match ends as soon as one of the wrestlers touches the mat with any part of his body other than the feet. This match will soon be over.

and try to break his opponent's balance with a quick sideways push.

Another maneuver is a quick pivot behind the opponent, followed by a strong push that drives him out of the ring. Remember, unlike other forms of martial arts, these moves are designed to end the match. That's the object of sumo—get a fast advantage and win the match.

Grabbing the Belt

Though a sumo doesn't wear much clothing, the thick loincloth, or **waist belt**, is fair game for the opponent. A strong sumo can actually grab the belt and lift his opponent off the ground. Then he can try one of several different ways to throw his opponent to the floor. Sumos sometimes try an over-the-hip throw similar to that in judo.

Grabbing the belt can also lead to a trip. The wrestler reaches down and grabs the loincloth of his opponent. He pulls the opponent toward him while stepping over the outside of the opponent's leg with his own. He locks his leg behind the opponent's amd sends the opponent to the ground with a strong backwards push.

A wrestler can also use his legs to step inside the opponent's leg. The wrestler hooks the leg from the inside and then tries to push the opponent down.

Other Maneuvers

There are still more ways to win a sumo match. Like the others, they involve breaking the opponent's balance so he can be pushed from the ring or thrown to the ground. When one wrestler charges, the other can try to sidestep. If the wrestler gets to the side or behind, he will have the advantage. From there, he can push and drive, or hook and trip.

One way to control the opponent is to lock his arm straight out, then make a pull or pushing move. Sumo wrestlers are very difficult to move, so this must be a strong and fast move.

Sumo wrestlers often use slaps and grabs to surprise an opponent and catch him off guard. One traditional maneuver involves a quick push to the throat of the opponent with both hands. This can cause the opponent to lose his balance. The wrestler can then charge and push his opponent from the ring. Or, it might distract his opponent's attention, allowing the wrestler to try a push, trip, or throw.

Wrestlers can slap and grab their opponents. Pushing, shoving, and tripping are also allowed.

In a way, sumo wrestling is on the edge of the martial arts. Unlike karate, kung fu, tae kwon do and others, it isn't practiced in many countries. And it hasn't really become popular in the United States and Canada. Matches are

very short and don't have the kind of dazzling spins and kicks of other martial arts.

But sumo wrestlers have great physical skills and great power. Sumo can be a way to test your power and quickness. It's also a contact sport that can help get you in condition for other sports. And, if done right, chances for injury are very small.

The Hawaiian wrestler Ozeki Konishiki prepares to enter the ring.

Glossary

aerobic exercise—an exercise such as running or swimming that improves stamina. It allows an athlete to perform longer without getting tired.

basho—the Japanese name for a sumo match

belt—the loin cloth worn by professional sumo wrestlers. The cloth is wrapped around the waist between four and seven times, giving it the appearance of a wide, thick belt.

grand champion—the highest ranking a professional sumo wrestler can achieve

mawashi—the Japanese name for the loincloth worn by sumo wrestlers

ring—the circle, 15 feet in diameter, in which a sumo wrestling match takes place

sumo charge—the way in which many sumo matches begin. Both wrestlers charge at each other with all the power they can muster. They hope to drive their opponent out of the ring and end the match quickly.

throws—moves designed to force the opponent to lose his balance and touch the floor of the ring

trips—moves designed to get the opponent to touch the floor of the ring

To Learn More

Barrett, Norman S. *Martial Arts.* New York: Franklin Watts, 1988.

Buckingham, Dorothea N. *The Essential Guide to Sumo.* Honolulu: Bess, 1994.

Long, Walter. *Sumo: A Pocket Guide.* Rutland, VT: Tuttle, 1989.

Reisberg, Ken. *The Martial Arts.* New York: Franklin Watts, 1979.

Ribner, Susan and Richard Chin. *The Martial Arts.* New York: Harper & Row, 1978.

Some Useful Addresses

Magazines

Sumo World
c/o Foreign Press Club
1-7-1 Yuraka-cho
Chiyoda-ku
Tokyo 100, Japan

Black Belt Magazine
24715 Avenue Rockefeller
Santa Clarita, CA 91380

Photo Credits
Cover: Paul J. Buklarewicz
Paul J. Buklarewicz: pgs. 6, 22, 28, 31, 40.
©Duomo/David Madison: pgs. 4, 14, 15, 22, 24, 25, 26, 36, 39.
©Cameramann Int'l, Ltd., pgs. 8, 10-11, 12, 13, 17, 18, 19, 21, 29, 32.

Index